Making Your Time Count

Emilie Barnes

Making Your Time Count

HARVEST HOUSE PUBLISHERS
Eugene, Oregon 97402

MAKING YOUR TIME COUNT

Taken from **MORE HOURS IN MY DAY**
Copyright © 1982 by Harvest House Publishers
Eugene, Oregon 97402

ISBN 0-89081-679-4

Printed in the United States of America.

Contents

Total Mess to Total Rest Chart

1

A LOVE STORY

✳

Emilie's Roots

I was raised in a Jewish home. My father was orphaned as a very young child in Vienna. As they often did with orphans, they placed him where he would learn a vocation. My father had the wonderful experience of being raised in the palace in Vienna in the kitchen. Later he came to America as a very fine Viennese chef. He met a beautiful young woman and they were married. But it wasn't until my mother was 38 years old that I was born, although I do have a brother who is a couple of years older than I.

When I was 11 years old my father became very ill with a coronary and passed away. We didn't have any insurance, so Mother was left with two almost-teenage children and a lot of debts to pay. She didn't know exactly what she was going to do, but I have an aunt and uncle who absolutely adored our little family. My aunt and uncle loaned my mother money to open a dress shop. Mom had a real flair for sewing and tailoring, so she opened this tiny dress shop, and we lived in three rooms behind the store.

At 11 years of age, I found myself beginning my education in domestic engineering. My mother began to teach me and train me, and I took on the responsibility of those three little rooms. I did the washing and ironing, I planned the meals, I prepared the meals, I shopped for the meals. While I was going to school my mother was teaching me the dress business, and I was very conscientious about it because I felt it was very important to help our family at that time. We were able to get ourselves out of debt and move to a larger location where we had a little apartment that was away from the dress shop.

The New Model

At that time I was about 15 years old. I had never had a date, and in fact I really didn't look at boys and boys didn't really look at me. One of the reasons was the way I looked. I had brown pigtails piled on top of my head with two big red bows. It isn't just any boy who wants to take out a girl who looks like a fire truck! About this time my mother decided she wanted to do some fashion shows in the local restaurant during the lunch hour. The cheapest way to get a model was to send her daughter, Emilie, off to modeling school. So one night a week I went to modeling school. You can imagine what they thought that first night when I walked in with two big red bows on top of my head! I'm sure they thought,

"If we can do something with her, our school is certainly going to be a success!"

While I was there I met a beautiful girl by the name of Esther. Esther was a natural beauty, a natural model. She would get on the ramp and just slither along, so graceful and charming and at ease. The rest of us would get on the ramp and just sort of klunk along after her.

One of the things I liked about Esther was that she was what you would call a boy-attracter. I thought that if I became good friends with her, maybe I could get a date.

And you know, that's exactly what happened! One evening we went to the local movie house, and, as many of the teenagers did during the intermission, we congregated in the lobby and introduced each other to our friends. I saw some friends I was going to school with, and I introduced them to Esther. They thought she was just beautiful and wanted to introduce her to some other friends who in turn introduced us to still other friends. This one particular young man looked at her and just couldn't take his eyes off her. The young man said to her, "I'd really like to take you out," but Esther said, "That'll be fine, but you'll have to get a date for my girl friend, Emilie." He took one look at me and said, "I'll give you a call, and I'll see what I can do." He called the next day and said, "You know, Esther, I just can't find a date for your girl friend, Emilie." She replied, "I'm sorry, then, but I won't be able to go out with you." He answered, "Well, I have an identical twin brother who owes me a favor. Maybe he'll take her out."

The Twin Brother

And, sure enough, his twin brother became my blind date. His name was Bob Barnes, and to this day he says that I was the date and he was blind. But that was the beginning of a marvelous summer romance. We had a wonderful time all summer long. We went beaching, bicycling, picnicking, and partying.

One evening, after Bob and I had been on a date, he brought me home and we sat down on the sofa in the living room. He got real serious as he took his hands and held my face in them. He looked me right in the eye and said, "Emilie, I love you, but I cannot ask you to marry me." I certainly couldn't understand that. I loved him and he loved me. Wasn't that the most important thing between two people? Then he said to me, "Emilie, you know that I'm a Christian." Well, I knew he was a Gentile, but a Christian? What was a Christian, anyway? Bob said to me, "A Christian is a person within whom Christ dwells." I replied, "Who is Christ?" And he answered, "Let me explain it to you this way, Emilie. If God wanted to communicate with His people, how would He do it? If there were a snail crawling along and you wanted to talk with that snail, how would you do it? You'd have to become a snail, wouldn't you?" He continued, "That's what God did. He became a Person in His Son, Jesus Christ. He came to this earth to love and teach His people." Then Bob added, "Emilie, most of all He came to die for our sins—your sins, and my sins, and the world's sins."

I looked at Bob Barnes and I said, "That's wonderful and that's fine, but I'm not a sinner." Some of you may recognize that you're sinners, but I had been a good girl all my life. I had minded my mother and done all the things I was supposed to do. I had been to Hebrew school and was confirmed. I was a good little Jewish girl. I believed in God. Then Bob said to me, "Do you know what sin is? Sin is when you say that you want to lead your own life, to go your own way, and make your own decisions, and not even acknowledge God for those decisions in your life." And that's exactly what I had been doing. I had been living my life for me, myself, and I.

Opening the Door

Then Bob said, "In Revelation 3:20, Christ says, 'Behold, I stand at the door and knock. If anyone hears my voice and opens the door, I'll come in. I'll fellowship with you and you can fellowship with Me.' Emilie, that doorknob is on the inside of your heart. You have to be the one to open it and invite Him to come in, and when you do, that's what makes you a Christian."

I knew that I loved Bob, and I knew he was the kind of man I wanted to marry, but I had to make some decisions of my own in my life. As he left that night, he told me that he loved me, that he would be praying for me, and that he would trust God for my life.

Well, I knew I was in love with Bob Barnes, and I knew that if I didn't become a Christian I wouldn't be able to marry the man I loved, but I was also smart enough to know that I couldn't just fake it and *say* I was a Christian the rest of my life. It would have to be real or not at all. So that night, as I went to bed, I said a prayer to God, in my own words, for the first time in my life. I said, "God, I don't understand all this, but if you did have a Son and His name is Jesus, and if He is the Messiah that our people are waiting for, then I want to open the door of my heart, and I want You to come in and dwell in me. But, God, I want You to prove it to me."

I thought I was going to get a letter from God in the mail the next day. But God doesn't always work that way, does He? I began to think that maybe it wasn't Bob Barnes that I was in love with: maybe it was Jesus Christ in him that was so special in this young man's life. During the many times I had been invited into their home, never once did his family say anything to me about being of a different faith. But they loved me and were concerned for me, and of course today I know that they were praying for me. They were praying that God would be revealing Himself in a mighty way in my life.

And it was happening. Miracles were happening and I didn't even recognize them. One was that my mother allowed to date a Gentile. The second miracle that happened in my life was that my mother allowed me to go to church with him.

Bob and Emilie

My aunt wanted me to marry a doctor or an

attorney, to live on a high hill, drive a big fancy car, and wear lots of diamonds. To her that was success. But success comes in other ways, doesn't it? And so she said to me, "Emilie, I'd like to send you to one of the finest finishing schools in Europe. I'd like to give you a car, a wardrobe, and an unlimited expense account if you'll not marry this young man." Well, that's everything in the world that a 16-year-old would love to have. But, it was at that very moment that God proved to me that I had in my heart God's free gift, our Messiah, Jesus Christ. And I was able to say to my sweet auntie, "I love you, but I'd like to marry the young man that I'm in love with, and together we're going to begin to establish a Christian home."

So Bob and I were married. I was starting my senior year in high school and he was starting his first year of teaching. In fact, he used to have to sign my report cards! Three years after we were married our daughter Jenny was born, and a few months after Jenny was born, we discovered that we were going to be parents to three more children. How were we going to do that? Well, my brother had gotten married and had had three precious little children. One day the mommy of these children walked out of the house and never came back. This absolutely destroyed my brother. But, God had a pattern for my life. God knew that the time was going to come when I needed every bit of experience that I had in taking care of a home and in handling responsibilities, because now I was going to become the mother of four children under four years old.

Five to Learn From

We took those precious little children into our home, and everything was fabulous. I had everything pulled together: I had those little kids spiffed up; I was making clothes for them; I did the washing, the ironing, and the food planning; and the house was in order. I was absolutely superwoman for about a month—until we discovered that I was pregnant. Number five. When our son Brad was born we had five children under five years old, and I was 21. But God has a pattern for our lives, and He knew that the day would come when I would be teaching women. Titus 2:3,4 tells us that the older women are to teach the younger women. Never in a million years did I think I would ever be an older woman, but I needed that experience. I needed to be able to identify with women today so that I'm able to say that I know what they're going through. I know the heartache, I know the weariness that they experience.

2

Daily Scheduling

✳

God really did a number on me when I was growing up, because He prepared me for being able to identify with you, to know that you have struggles in your lives, and to help you become organized.

How do you take care of your children and your husband and still keep your priorities in order and glorify the Lord? It's difficult. There's no doubt about it. So we're going to talk about how we can actually have more hours in our day.

The Night Worker

We're going to start with our daily routine. In Proverbs 31:17,18 God tells us that the virtuous woman is energetic and a hard worker, watches for bargains, and works far into the night. If we work far into the night, I guess that means we're going to have to start the night before in order to get ourselves together for the following day. Some of you are saying, "I've got a 24-hour job."

You do, absolutely. If you have children at home, you are working 24 hours a day. Some of you were probably up three or four times last night with a sick baby. There's no doubt that God knows what He's talking about when He says you work far into the night. If you're a working woman, your time is especially short at home, but being organized will help free you from guilt feelings about a messy home. So we're going to start the night before.

The Laundry Game

One of the ways in which you can do this is by gathering your laundry and sorting it out. A lot of these things you should teach your children to do. I encourage you to do that.

Take a piece of fabric (something with a lot of color in it) and make a laundry bag about 20 inches wide by 36 inches high. You might want to use a king-sized pillowcase with a shoelace strung through the top. Then say to your little one, "Okay, we're going to play a game."

Don't tell them it's work. By the time they're ten they realize you've been working them to death, but they don't know it when they're little, so don't tell them. Say, "We're going to play a game, and it's called Sort the Laundry." Then get out your laundry bag with lots of colors and say, "This is the bag where all the dirty clothes that have a lot of colors go. Now find something in this dirty-clothes pile that has a lot of colors." So they run over and pick it up, and you say, "Right!

Now put it in the colored laundry bag." So they put it in there.

Then make a bag that is navy blue or dark brown and tell them, "This is where all the dark-colored clothes go. Run over and find something that's dark colored." You see, you're playing a game with them. They do it, and you say, "Great! That's absolutely right!" Then you make a bag that's all white, and you say, "Now this is where the white dirty clothes go—the white T-shirts, the white socks, the white underwear, and those things."

What you're doing is teaching a four-year-old to sort the laundry. When they're six and seven and ten, do you ever have to teach them again? No, because you've already taught them once. Somebody once said to me, "Well, when they're 15 you have to teach them again, because when they're 15 they don't want to do anything. They're that weird teenage group." But at least they know how to do it, and they'll come back to it again later on.

Another thing I did which really worked out well was to make individual laundry bags for each of the kids to hang in their room behind their door or in their closet. (The other three colored laundry bags go by your washing machine.) I made individual bags that were very colorful and matched the kids' rooms. This is where they put their own dirty clothes. Then whoever had the job of sorting the laundry for the week collected everybody's laundry bag and sorted the laundry by color.

The Daily Work Planner Chart

Now take a good look at the Daily Work Planner Chart. First, our family would write out all the chores for the week on slips of paper and put them into a basket. Then we would go around one by one, allowing the children to pick out a chore. It was like a little game: whatever they chose was the chore they had to do for the week. And it went on the Daily Work Planner Chart.

Now, you see, this relieves you because they don't get mad at you. They can't say, "Golly, how come I have to do this one again?" They chose it—it was their own fault. So they have to live with it for a week. Notice that Mom and Dad are listed on the chart too. What that shows the kids is that you're working together as a family. At the end of the day, when everyone's checked their charts and done their chores as best they can, put a little happy face on the chart. Put on a Christmas tree if it's Christmas, or a little Easter cross if it's Easter. At the end of the week you check your chart and say, "You know, our family did a fantastic job this week. We're going to have a picnic at the park, or go bicycling together, or have an evening with popcorn because we've really worked well together in accomplishing this." Do you see what that's doing? It's uniting the home and family.

Setting the Table

Another chore that can be delegated is setting the breakfast table the night before. A

DAILY WORK PLANNER CHART

DAY OF THE WEEK	MOM	DAD	#1 CHILD	#2 CHILD	#3 CHILD	#4 CHILD	#5 CHILD
SATURDAY							
SUNDAY							
MONDAY							
TUESDAY							
WEDNESDAY							
THURSDAY							
FRIDAY							

five-year-old can learn to set the table. It amazed me when our daughter Jenny brought her friends home at 16 or 17 years of age and they didn't know where the knife, fork, and spoon went. It wasn't their fault, though. It was because Mom or Dad never took the time to teach them. As the five-year-old sets the table the night before, you can say, "Okay, Timmy, do whatever you want. You can use Mom's good china, or you can use paper plates, or you can have candlelight, or you can put your favorite teddy bear on the table. I don't care—whatever you want to do."

I think that too many times we put the good china on the table only for company and at Christmas. Who are the most important people in our life? Our family! And yet we seldom use the good china for those people who mean the very most to us. We can't take the china with us, so if a piece gets broken here and there, it gets broken. I would rather have my children be able to enjoy the nicer things, and to use them and live with them, than to have them in a china cabinet where they can't be enjoyed. So I say let them have the freedom to be able to use their good china, and teach them as you go along.

The Weekly Calendar

Now notice the Weekly Calendar. On this calendar list those things which are going to go on for the week. Suzie has to go to the orthodontist, Timmy has football practice, and Bessie has Brownies. You can feel free now because you

WEEKLY CALENDAR

DAY OF WEEK	MONDAY	TUESDAY	WEDNESDAY	THURSDAY	FRIDAY	SATURDAY	SUNDAY
MORNING							
NOON							
NIGHT							

know where you're needed and where you're children will have to be. You check it over and fill it out the night before so you'll know what's happening the next day. Also fill in your work schedule if you work outside your home. Then your family can see it and know what's going on.

We women have to get up early because, even though we have all the modern appliances, we still don't seem to have enough time. Why? Because we're not using them effectively and efficiently. We have to get our homes organized, and for some of us that may mean getting up at five o'clock in the morning. If I were to ask you if you made your bed today, what would you answer? How long does it take to make a bed? About two minutes. So what's two minutes out of a whole day to make a bed?

I have a friend who never made her bed. She figured she would just get in it again at night, so why bother to make it? Now she has a son who is 20 years old and is an absolute slob. He's never made his bed because he never had an example. He doesn't know how to put a thing away. It's not really his fault, though, because Mom never took the time to teach him to make his own bed and take care of his room.

Helping Them Come to Breakfast

After we make the bed we're going to get into the kitchen. (We can get the first load of wash in beforehand if we like.) God tells us several times in the Bible that we can't be lazy as women.

Then we get breakfast cooked and call everyone to the table for breakfast, but they don't come. Isn't that irritating? I think that was one of the things that bothered me the most. I said to the children, "We're going to have a meeting." I continued, "You know I've really got a problem. I call you children for breakfast but you don't come. Now is there anything you might suggest that could help with this problem?" So they said to me, "Golly, Mom, if you'd just let us know a couple of minutes before breakfast is ready, we'd come right to the table." So that's what we did.

Another thing—serve everyone at one time, and don't be a short-order cook. I may be a Christian today, but I'm still Jewish. I want to please everybody because I'm still that good little Jewish mother. So I was fixing French toast for Brad and omelets and pancakes for Jenny. But what happened to me? I got exhausted. I thought, "This cannot go on."

The Weekly Menu Planner

I came up with a chart I called the Weekly Menu Planner. I would have a different breakfast every day, but everyone would eat the same thing every morning. So when Brad came to the table and said, "Ick, I hate oatmeal," I replied to him, "Okay, so you don't like oatmeal. Tomorrow morning, as you see on the Menu Planner, we're going to have French toast, and that's your very favorite." So at least one morning a week we pleased at least one of the children. This worked so beautifully that I decided to extend the idea and make menus for the whole week. Also, I

WEEKLY MENU PLANNER

DAY OF WEEK	MONDAY	TUESDAY	WEDNESDAY	THURSDAY	FRIDAY	SATURDAY	SUNDAY
BREAKFAST							
LUNCH							
DINNER							

tried a new menu at least once a week. That added a little variety.

After I made out my menus I listed everything I needed at the market in order to prepare the meals for that week. What happens when you do this? You won't buy things you don't need. You save money and you feel organized because you know you have your meals planned. You shop wisely and have everything in the house that is going to be in those meals for the week.

Back to Breakfast

At breakfast ask each family member, "Where am I going to be needed today?" Check your Weekly Calendar as you go over the day's plans with them.

Then have everyone take their dishes to the kitchen sink. We had a rule in our family that no one ever left the table empty-handed. Each person always had to pick something up and take it to the sink. I would fill up the sink with hot, sudsy water, and then each person would put all their things into the water, where they would stay until I was ready to get back to them. Now what is this doing? It's saving work for you. It's saving you steps so you have energy to do other things that are more important.

Now say farewell to your family, because it's time for the children and family to be getting off to school or work. Proverbs 31:26 says, "When she speaks, her words are wise, and kindness is the rule for everything she says" (TLB). In the morning, when things are hassled and we're moving around quickly because we've got to get the children ready for school, we can become very irritated. Also, we had to make the bed this morning, and we're not really used to doing that. But at this point say to your husband, "Honey, is there anything I can do for you today?" He'll fall over in a dead faint the first morning you ask him, but then he will probably come up with a nice list of things the next day.

Then quickly check each child's room with him or her. Also, quickly check the bathrooms, and have the children wipe the toothpaste off the mirror. Once or twice a week you might want to go in and do a really good job, but get them used to cleaning up after themselves so they won't think you're a maid. Then, as they're leaving the house, check to see if they have their lunch, their lunch money, their books, their homework, and their gym clothes.

God says in Proverbs 31:17 that the virtuous woman is energetic and a hard worker. So we gals can't fall back into bed, can we? Besides, the bed is made, so it's not quite so tempting to get back into it! We have to keep going, get the second load of wash in and the dishes done. Now we can check our Menu Planner to see what we're going to have for dinner tonight and make sure we've taken what we need out of the freezer. Then we get our counters cleaned up and water our houseplants, and we rejoice that our basic housework is done and it's only 9:00 in the morning.

The Right Priorities

God tells us in Proverbs 31:27-30, "She watches carefully all that goes on throughout her household, and is never lazy. Her children stand and bless her; so does her husband. He praises her with these words: There are many fine women in the world, but you are the best of them all!" (TLB).

How do we receive that kind of praise from our children and our husband? There's only one way I know that will cause them to give us that genuine kind of praise, and that's by having our priorities as Christian women in order.

Do you know what our priorities should be? God tells us in Matthew 6:33 (KJV), "Seek ye first the kingdom of God and his righteousness; and all these things shall be added unto you." Our number one priority is God. There have been times in my life when I got my priorities out of order. There was a time when I needed to have a special time with my Lord, but the only time available was at 5:00 in the morning, when the house was still. And that was hard, because I might have been up three times during the night with the children. But I got up and spent that little time. I committed my works to the Lord, and my plans were established (Proverbs 16:3).

The Other Priorities

Our second priority is our husband. Our third priority is our children. Our fourth priority is our home. And number five is all the other things. That means helping a philanthropic group, being a Brownie leader, leading a Bible study, having luncheons out with the ladies, and shopping. I'll never forget the day my husband came to me and said, "Emilie, you love those children more than you do me." I said, "They need me. I have to do all these things for them." But in my heart I knew he was right.

God tells us that our children will stand and bless us, and so will our husbands, as long as we get our priorities in order. So remember that God is there. He's given those children to you as a gift. He's going to take care of them for you. Keep them in the right priority. Remember that you were a wife to your husband before you were a mother to your children.

Evening Time

Right now it's five o'clock and a zoo around the house. There's spilled milk all over the kitchen floor, and something's boiling over on the stove. The dog and cat are hungry and nipping at your heels. You've got kids all around you. Then the phone rings. And you're supposed to have a quiet and gentle spirit? It's tough, isn't it?

Did you know what I did at times like this? I just went into the bathroom, closed the door, and put my head in the potty. I said, "Lord, You said that I need a quiet and gentle spirit. So I'm asking for it." Then I went back out, and do you know what? I didn't get it. So I went back into the bathroom again and said, "You know, God, I didn't get it. You don't know what it's like out there." Sometimes I had to go back and forth two or three times. But eventually my heart was quieted and I was able to pull the kids together and organize them as best as I could.

Then I would be ready for my husband's arrival. When I heard his car coming up the driveway, I would drop everything and go to greet him. Now I know you're diapering that baby, but throw a diaper over him and go and greet your husband. What does it tell him when you run to the door to greet him as he comes in from work? You're telling him that he's important to you. You don't know what happened at work today— whether he had to fire his best friend, or the construction job fell through. So go to the door, greet him, throw your arms around him. Tell him that you're happy he's home, that you're thankful he's worked hard all day and provided for this home, for you and your children. Then let him have a few minutes to unwind with the paper or the mail or whatever. Try not to share the negative parts of the day with him until after dinner.

Then enjoy your family. God has given that family to you as a gift.

3

TOTAL MESS TO TOTAL REST

✳

Suppose I were to say to you, "Today I'm going to come home with you. I want you to take me into your house, and I want to go through your closets, look under your bed, open your drawers, look in your pantry, and go anyplace in your house. I just want to check out your house really good."

Some of you would reply, "Well, that's okay. I've got my house in order, and things are really good there, so you can come over." Others of you would say, "Okay, but don't go into the third bedroom, because I've been shoving things in that back bedroom for a long time. That's my little hideaway." Still others of you might say, "There is no way anybody is going to come into my house, because the whole place is a total mess!"

Controlling Your Home

Now I'm going to show you how to take that mess, no matter what size it is, and turn it into a home that you'll be able to maintain and rest in. You will control your home instead of your home controlling you.

Here's some equipment you'll need in order to work out this program. I'll tell you how to use this equipment later. You'll need three to ten boxes with lids, 16" deep by 12" wide by 10" high. You'll need a 3" x 5" card-file box and some 3" x 5" card files. I like to use the colored files because sometimes it's easier to remember the color than what you've written on the tab. Get ten cards in each color—blue, yellow, white, green, orange, cherry. Be sure to get some little tabs for each section of cards, and also a pen to write on them. Then you'll need at least ten colored file folders. (I like to use the colored ones because they help to identify things.) If you already have a metal file cabinet at home, that's great, but most people don't have one. The file boxes are a lot less expensive.

I've been teaching home organization seminars for several years now, and after about the first six months I discovered something about us women. Our intentions are good and we want to get started, but somehow we can't seem to get organized enough to get ourselves organized, and we just throw the whole program out the window. So pray about the program. Ask God to make you willing to get the materials and to incorporate them into your home.

Commit Yourself

You'll want to commit yourself to five weeks

in taking that total mess and cleaning it up. I don't want you to become overwhelmed thinking about it, because you're going to take a small portion at a time—only one room a week for the next five weeks. You'll do it nice and slow, so that you'll gradually get your home under control.

Now take three large boxes, or, if you prefer, three large trash bags. I like the trash bags because they're lightweight and you can drag them through the house. So take your three trash bags and label one of them "Put Away," one "Throw Away," and one "Give Away."

Now imagine yourself standing at the front door with these three big trash bags. Ring the doorbell, then walk through the front door. The first room you come to will be the first room you're going to clean. (If the kitchen is the room you walk into first, put it aside until the fifth week, because you'll need all the experience you can get by the time you get to the kitchen.) To make it easy, let's say we step into the living room, and on our right is the entry closet.

So we open up the entry closet. We're now going to take everything out of that entry closet. We have to get kind of vicious in making choices about what to do with all the stuff we've taken out of the closet. I recommend that you call on a friend who would like to help you with your house (and you with her house). It's great to have a friend because she'll help you make decisions that you haven't been able to make for 15 years. She'll tell you, "Throw it out or give it away," and that will be very helpful to you.

The Entry Closet

Now, we're going to put back into the entry closet all those things which actually belong in an entry closet. These include sweaters, coats, umbrella, boots, football blanket, binoculars, and tennis racket.

But now we have all these other things that don't belong in there, such as old magazines that we've collected for six or seven years. (We were going to look through them some rainy day and cut out the pictures and recipes, but we never did.) So we have to get rid of these things. We've also got papers and receipts and all sorts of other things in that entry closet, so we'll put these either in the Put Away bag, the Throw Away bag, or the Give Away bag.

As we go through our home every week for the next five weeks, we begin to fill up these bags. At the end of the fifth week we may have three, ten, or 15 bags full of various things. Then we put twisties on the trash bags marked Throw Away and set them out for the trash man. Now they're gone!

So now you have two bags left, the Give Away bag and the Put Away bag. The Give Away bag will hold things that maybe you want to hand down to some other family member or to relatives. Or it might include clothing that you want to give to a thrift shop, or sell at a rummage sale, or donate to your church.

Maybe you want to co-op—three or four of you who have done the five-week program may want to have a garage sale and make a little extra money to buy something for yourself or for the house, or to give to your church or missionary group.

Keeping It Neat

Now we have our house totally clean. But how are we going to maintain it that way? We certainly never want to go through this total mess again! The cleanup was enough to do for five weeks, and we don't *have* to do it again.

The way we maintain our house now is to take our 3" x 5" cards and label each of the tabs. The first color is going to be labeled "Daily." On these cards we list all those things that we have to do daily in our house in order to maintain it, such as washing the dishes and making the beds.

The second section is those things we do weekly. For example, on Monday we wash, on Tuesday we iron and water the houseplants, on Wednesday we mop the floors, on Thursday we vacuum and do our marketing, and so on through the week.

So now Thursday comes along, and Sue, your very special friend, calls you and says, "Let's go to lunch and go shopping. The department store has a big sale today." So you check your cards and say, "I've done all my daily things, but it's Thursday, so I have to vacuum and go to the market. I can do my marketing this afternoon when we get back from lunch, but I don't know about the vacuuming."

You go with Sue and get your bargains, but the vacuuming isn't done. So you decide to move the vacuuming over to Friday. But you look on Friday's card and see all those other things to do on Friday. So you take Friday's chores and move them to Saturday. But on Saturday you're going to the park with the kids. So you decide to move those things to *Sunday* now. But on Sunday you can't do them either because you're going to church and you've also got company coming afterward. So here you are going around in circles again. You've moved one job from day to day, but you're completely confused.

So don't do that. Instead, on Thursday, when you go to lunch with Sue and don't have time to vacuum, you move your vacuuming card to the back of the file. This means you don't vacuum your house again until next Thursday, when the vacuuming card comes up in your file again. In other words, you rotate your cards daily whether you do the allotted jobs or not.

This means that you're crunching along on dirty carpet for a week or two. You say, "I can't possibly do that." But now you're disciplining yourself to keep your priorities in order. So next week, when Sue calls and says, "Let's go to lunch," you'll tell her, "I'll go to lunch if I get my vacuuming done, because if I don't get it done today it means another whole week before I can do it." Remember, *you* want to be in control of your home, and not the other way around.

Next you have your monthly things. During Week #1 you clean the refrigerator. (You have a whole week to do it, or you can delegate the job to a child.) During Week #2 you clean the oven, and so forth. This way, every week you're doing a little bit to maintain your home so you never have to go through that total mess program again. Next you have quarterly things to do such as straightening drawers. Then you have biannual things to do (rearranging furniture, washing curtains). Finally there are the annual things, such as cleaning the basement, attic, and garage.

Your last tab, at the very back of your file, is your storage tab. Here you take your 3" x 5" card files and number them Box 1, Box 2, Box 3 and so forth. Then you take your storage boxes that you've been collecting (or that you've purchased), line them all up, and number them Box 1, Box 2, Box 3, and so on. You've got all these boxes in a row now, and a card that corresponds with each box.

Remember that Put Away bag, with Billy's first baby blanket? Well, you put all these things into Box 1. Then you list on the 3" x 5" card labeled Box 1 all the things which are actually in the box. And you do that with all the things you find in those Put Away bags.

So what have we done? We've taken that total mess and changed it into total rest. And we'll maintain that rest, with no guilt feelings about an unorganized house.

Total Mess to Total Rest Chart

Ask yourself, "How clean does my house have to be to keep my family happy?"

Equipment Needed

3 to 10 boxes with lids (tops)
3" x 5" card file
3" x 5" colored cards with dividers with colored tags
File box and file folders

How to Get Organized

A. Begin by collecting boxes with lids (tops).

B. Plan a 5-week program project.

C. Label 3 large boxes or trash bags as follows:
   1. Put Away
   2. Throw Away
   3. Give Away

D. Start at your front door and go through your house, starting with the living room and ending with the kitchen.
   1. Closets, drawers, shelves
   2. Get vicious!

Household Routine

A. Set up a 3" x 5" card file with dividers.

B. Label dividers in this card file as follows:
1. Daily 5. Biannually
2. Weekly 6. Annually
3. Monthly 7. Storage
4. Quarterly

C. Make a list of jobs:
1. Daily:
   a. Dishes
   b. Make beds
   c. Clean bathrooms
   d. Pick up rooms
   e. Pick up kitchen

2. Weekly:
   a. Monday—laundry, marketing
   b. Tuesday—iron, water plants
   c. Wednesday—mop floors
   d. Thursday—vacuum, shopping
   e. Friday—change bed linens
   f. Saturday—yardwork
   g. Sunday—free except to plan for next week

NOTE: If you skip a job on an allotted day, **don't do it—skip it until next week and put card in the back of the file.**

3. Monthly:
   a. Week #1 —clean refrigerator
   b. Week #2 —clean oven
   c. Week #3 —mending
   d. Week #4 —clean and dust baseboards

4. Quarterly:
   a. Drawers, windows
   b. Closets, move furniture, and vacuum
   c. China cabinets, cupboards

5. Biannually:
   a. Screens
   b. Rearrange furniture

6. Annually:
   a. Wash curtains
   b. Clean drapes
   c. Clean carpets
   d. Wash walls

Storage

A. Get boxes with tops and number each box.

B. Assign each box a 3" x 5" card with corresponding number. For example:
   Box #1 —a. Bill's baby clothes
           b. Bill's baby book
   Box #2 —Toys
   Box #3 —Seasonal clothes
   Box #4 —Christmas decorations
   Box #5 —Books: high school yearbooks, materials
   Box #6 —Scrapbooks
   Box #7 —Old pictures
   Box #8 —Snow clothes
   Box #9 —Scrap fabrics

C. File box with file folders—label as follows:
   1. Report cards
   2. Appliance instructions
   3. Warranties
   4. Decorating ideas
   5. Insurance papers and booklets
   6. Special notes, letters, cards
   7. Car repair receipts
   8. Receipts from purchases such as furniture and antiques

Harvest Pocket Books

These compact pocket books are excerpted from best-selling, full-length Harvest House books. Each booklet gives the major thrust of the complete book in an inexpensive, condensed version, designed for readers on the go. Further material on each topic can be obtained by purchasing the full-length edition.

Dear Reader:

We would appreciate hearing from you regarding this Harvest House pocket book. It will enable us to continue to give you the best in Christian publishing.

1. What most influenced you to purchase *Making Your Time Count*?
   - ☐ Author
   - ☐ Subject matter
   - ☐ Backcover copy
   - ☐ Recommended
   - ☐ Cover/Title
   - ☐ _____

2. Your overall rating of this book:
   - ☐ Excellent ☐ Very good ☐ Good ☐ Fair ☐ Poor

3. How likely would you be to purchase other books by this author?
   - ☐ Very likely
   - ☐ Somewhat likely
   - ☐ Not very likely
   - ☐ Not at all

4. After reading this Harvest House Pocket Book would you be inclined to purchase the complete book, *More Hours in My Day*?
   - ☐ Yes ☐ No

5. What types of books most interest you? (check all that apply)
   - ☐ Women's Books
   - ☐ Marriage Books
   - ☐ Current Issues
   - ☐ Self Help/Psychology
   - ☐ Bible Studies
   - ☐ Fiction
   - ☐ Biographies
   - ☐ Children's Books
   - ☐ Youth Books
   - ☐ Other _____

6. Please check the box next to your age group.
   - ☐ Under 18 ☐ 25-34 ☐ 45-54
   - ☐ 18-24 ☐ 35-44 ☐ 55 and over

Mail to: Editorial Director
Harvest House Publishers
1075 Arrowsmith
Eugene, OR 97402

Name _____

Address _____

City _____ State _____ Zip _____

Thank you for helping us to help you in future publications!